Foreword

I believe I have seen every important motion picture made in the last forty years and in my opinion BEN-HUR may well set a new standard for years to come. It is not only a notable contribution to the art of motion pictures but it is my sincere belief that it approaches the ultimate in dramatic entertainment in any medium. It will be remembered as an enjoyable and rewarding experience, not merely as a great motion picture. This may sound extravagant, but you have seen, or surely will see BEN-HUR. The judgment will be yours.

I should like to pay tribute to those persons who poured into this great motion picture their utmost in industry, devotion, talent and skills.

First, General Lew Wallace, who wrote the novel. Few books have exerted such a world-wide influence on so many millions.

Then the producer, Sam Zimbalist, who saw in BEN-HUR the crowning of his life's work. Tragically he died during the final weeks of production. Truly no man could have given more of himself. I wish he were here to see the results of his work.

With equal dedication and superb artistry, Director William Wyler, whose magical perception in evoking and reflecting human emotions was never so supremely tested or so tellingly shown; and ranging over the entire enterprise—Sol Siegel, the Metro-Goldwyn-Mayer Studio production head. His standards of good taste and sense of entertainment values are always evident.

Karl Tunberg, the only Hollywood writer twice nominated as a Rhodes Scholar, is the author of the screen play. His magnificent script reflects his deep perception and fine literary skill. Other great writers also worked on "BEN-HUR," including S. N. Behrman, Maxwell Anderson, Gore Vidal and Christopher Fry. They found in "BEN-HUR" a challenge to their finest creative writing.

The musical score by Miklos Rozsa, whose qualifications for this task are unsurpassed, is moving and beautiful.

Finally, a warm salute to the thousands I have not named here who, drawing strength from the magnificence of the undertaking in which they were engaged, gave their abilities in full measure.

We at M-G-M feel pride, a justifiable one we believe, in placing this great "Tale of The Christ" before the public.

Jos R Vogel

President,
Metro-Goldwyn-Mayer Pictures

From
Metro-Goldwyn-Mayer

BEN-HUR

A Tale of the Christ

by General Lew Wallace

A Random House Book

A FABULOUS STORY....

AN IMMORTAL HERO....

A FANTASTIC AUTHOR....

FOR eighty years, the story of *Ben-Hur* has never been out of print. Probably no other novel has ever had such influence on so many millions around the world. In the title, *Ben-Hur,* there seems to be the magic that stirs the heart and uplifts the soul. About once every twenty years since 1880, *Ben-Hur* has roared over the literary and theatrical horizon to create a new global furor.

All of this began when a man of war decided to write about the Prince of Peace. In the eyes of critics, he was not a great writer; by his own admission he was not a deeply religious man. Yet, as he wrote, seated under a beech tree in Crawfordsville, Indiana, his pen dipped into purple ink, there must have come to him some inspiration; some force must have formed his thoughts and shaped his words. How else can one explain the appeal of his novel, completed some eight years later? How else could he have composed a story that, as one literary historian reported, "brought millions to their feet to cheer and more millions to their knees to pray?"

General Lew Wallace, flamboyant hero of the Civil War, lived a fantastic life. He could have written about his adventures on the battlefields. He could have found a novel in his contact with Billy the Kid and other desperadoes who ruled the Territory of New Mexico during his days as Governor of that frontier territory. He might have written exotic tales of his days as U.S. Minister to Turkey.

But he chose to let his thoughts roam from the tranquility of his Indiana home to the Holy Land which he had never seen, thousands of miles and thousands of years away.

He selected the turbulent times of the pagan Roman Empire and that period of history which influenced all mankind—the years between the birth of Christ and His crucifixion.

General Wallace, always an optimist, told his wife, back in 1880, that it was quite possible *Ben-Hur* would provide them with as much as $100 a year in royalties! He lived to see his book return greater royalties than any other novel had ever earned. There came a time when he negotiated a "million dollar" deal for the stage rights; and his heirs arranged another "million dollar" contract for the silent screen rights.

This statue of General Lew Wallace, lawyer, soldier, statesman and author of Ben-Hur, stands in the Hall of Statuary at the United States Capitol in Washington, D.C.

THIS BOOK WAS PRODUCED BY RAY FREIMAN

This is a photograph of the rescue scene in the original Broadway play. Stagehands stood in the wings holding pieces of cloth and shaking them to simulate waves. Quite a contrast to the dramatic sea sequence in the film!

Since Wallace's death, in 1905, *Ben-Hur* has become recognized as one of the most valuable theatrical properties in the history of show business. And today *Ben-Hur* has become a "best-seller" once again. No less than a dozen publishers now have new editions of the novel on book shelves and in the libraries.

For years, General Wallace refused to permit dramatization of his book. He finally yielded and in November, 1899 Klaw & Erlanger revealed to a startled, cheering Broadway the first stage production of *Ben-Hur*. For twenty years, the play ran on and on, touring hundreds of American cities and circling the globe. The original two chariots, on treadmills, became five, then eight chariots; numerous "Ben-Hurs" and "Messalas" played the leads, beginning with William Farnum and William S. Hart, long before they became film stars. Wherever *Ben-Hur* played, there was a frenzied response. Babies were named for the hero of the day; merchandise adopted *Ben-Hur* as a trade name; schools studied the book; churches heard sermons on it.

In 1926, the silent screen version of *Ben-Hur* again made theatre history. The lavish $4,000,000 production was a milestone in the development of the screen. That picture might still be running if talking pictures had not replaced the silent screen.

Now, all this is happening again. A great wave of interest in *Ben-Hur* is sweeping the nation and the world. With the modern magic of the motion picture art, *Ben-Hur* promises to reach a new pinnacle of public acclaim.

William S. Hart (left) as Messala and William Farnum as Ben-Hur in the early stage production. Later both of these performers gained fame in motion pictures.

BEN HUR *is a story of people ... as human as any you know today.... the rich, the poor, the cruel, the kind. The lovers and the loved, the haters and the hated. Men of violence and men of peace .... people of every kind, whose lives become entwined with that of the prince who became a slave.*

Judah Ben-Hur

Prince of Judea, who challenged the evil might of pagan Rome.

CHARLTON HESTON, who was born in Evanston, Illinois, and is a graduate of Northwestern University. He began his professional acting career in radio and made his Broadway debut with Katharine Cornell in "Antony and Cleopatra." Has starred in a number of stage plays and television dramas. During the past 10 years has appeared in twenty important motion pictures, including "The Greatest Show on Earth," "The Big Country" and "The Ten Commandments," in which he portrayed Moses.

Esther

The Beautiful, whose love was stronger than the bonds of slavery.

HAYA HARAREET, who was born in Haifa, Palestine, and lived most of her life in Tel-Aviv. While serving the required two years in her country's armed forces, she began acting in service shows. Once out of uniform, she joined Tel-Aviv's Chambre Theatre and acted in dozens of plays. Speaks five languages fluently and won the feminine lead in BEN-HUR after William Wyler remembered having met her briefly at the Cannes Film Festival and ordered her tested.

Drawings of *Ben-Hur's* Cast of Characters are the work of Joseph J. Smith, native Philadelphian and graduate of the Pennsylvania Museum School of Industrial Art. Mr. Smith has become one of the most famous artists in Hollywood.

Quintus Arrius

Admiral of the Roman Fleet, a deadly enemy but a steadfast friend.

JACK HAWKINS, who was born in London and has been acting since the age of thirteen. He made his professional debut in the original production of Shaw's "Saint Joan," and at eighteen was an established British stage star. He also starred on Broadway in a number of plays. Among his more recent important films have been "The Fallen Idol," "The Cruel Sea" and "The Bridge on the River Kwai."

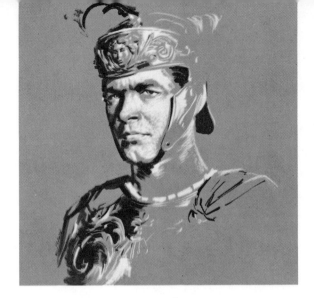

Messala

The Roman Warrior, who traded loyalty for power and trust for treachery.

STEPHEN BOYD, who was born and educated in Belfast, Ireland. Made his acting debut at the age of eight in a BBC broadcast and at eighteen joined the Ulster Dramatic Group. In London, actor Michael Redgrave helped him get his start with the Windsor Repertory Company. His portrayal of the Irish agent in the film "The Man Who Never Was," led him to Hollywood and ultimately to BEN-HUR.

Sheik Ilderim

The Lusty Sheik, he believed one God and fifty wives enough for any man.

HUGH GRIFFITH, the Welsh star of London and Broadway stage. Born on the Isle of Anglesey in North Wales, he began acting in amateur theatricals while a bank clerk in London. Following six wartime years in uniform, joined Shakespeare Memorial Theatre at Stratford-on-Avon. Has starred in scores of films and plays and his recent portrayal of the father in the original Broadway production of "Look Homeward, Angel" won him wide acclaim.

Miriam

The Loving, all the cruelties of Rome could not destroy her faith.

MARTHA SCOTT, who was born in Jamesport, Missouri, and is a graduate of the University of Michigan. She began her career with the Civic Theatre in Detroit, has since starred in a number of plays, including the original production of "Our Town." Among her outstanding films have been "Cheers for Miss Bishop," "One Foot in Heaven," "So Well Remembered," "The Ten Commandments" and "Sayonara." Miss Scott gave up her own network show on TV to be in BEN-HUR.

Tirzah

The Outcast, condemned to a living death by the man she loved.

CATHY O'DONNELL, who was born in Siluria, Alabama and educated in Greensboro, Alabama. Majored in drama at Oklahoma City University, made debut on stage in "Life With Father," and left cast to enter films as the wife of the armless sailor in "The Best Years of Our Lives." Since then has had leading roles in many motion pictures, including "Your Red Wagon," "Bury Me Dead," "They Live By Night," "The Miniver Story" and "Twisted Road."

SAM JAFFE, who was born in New York City and began acting career at seventeen by playing five different characters in a one-act playlet for the Bronx Cultural Institute. His talent and versatility led him to the Washington Square Players, the Ben Greet Shakespearean Company, and to leads in a long list of Broadway plays. Made screen debut in "Ace of Aces" in 1933 and has since appeared prominently in more than a score of films, including "Lost Horizon," "Gunga Din," "Gentlemen's Agreement," and "The Asphalt Jungle."

Simonides

The Penniless Slave, who ruled empire of fabulous wealth.

Balthasar

The Wise Man, who followed the star and found Man's Hope.

FINLAY CURRIE, who was born in Edinburgh, Scotland, and became intrigued by the theatre while studying music at Edinburgh University. He joined the Edinburgh Stock Company; toured America in 1899 with Lew Dockstader's Minstrel Show. Has toured the world playing countless roles in a wide variety of plays and films. Among the latter have been "Great Expectations," "Quo Vadis," "Treasure Island," and "Ivanhoe."

MARINA BERTI, who was born in London of a British mother and an Italian father. Has spent most of her life in Italy, where she has starred in many Italian films. Portrayed ill-fated slave girl, Eunice, in "Quo Vadis." Devotes most of her time to her husband and two sons, making only a rare appearance in an important film production.

Flavia

The Wanton, whose beauty w the trap set for Ben-Hur.

Pontius Pilate

The Corrupt, judged all men by himself and condemned them.

FRANK THRING, who was born in Melbourne, Australia, where his father owned a number of theatres and radio stations. Began acting in radio, but later switched to the stage, making his debut in "Henry VIII" at age of nineteen. Formed own acting company and took it to London. Appeared at Stratford-on-Avon in "Titus Andronicus"; later toured Europe with Olivier in this Shakespearean drama. Made motion picture debut in "The Vikings." BEN-HUR marks his second film appearance.

ANDRE MORELL, who was born in London. Joined a repertory company in Somerset while still a young man; made London debut in "Call It a Day" in 1936. Since his film debut in "Thirteen Men and a Gun" in 1938, has had prominent roles in more than forty motion pictures, including "The Bridge on the River Kwai"; now divides time between stage, screen and TV

Sextus
The Failure, who found Roman power no match for simple faith.

GEORGE RELPH, often called the Grand Old Gentleman of the British theatre, who was born at Cullercoats, Northumberland, England. Made first appearance at the Theatre Royal, Grimsby, in 1905 in "Othello"; has since starred in more than sixty plays. Toured Australia in 1909; appeared on Broadway in "Kismet" in 1911; joined a stock company in Boston, and later appeared in Paris and many other cities. Has played leading roles in scores of motion pictures.

Tiberius
Emperor, who ruled Rome
hen Rome ruled the world.

TERENCE LONGDEN, who was born in Newark-on-Trent, Nottingham, England. Joined Royal Academy of Dramatic Arts after serving in naval air corps in World War II. Made hit on London stage in "Treasure Hunt" and "Red Letter Day"; later toured Australia and New Zealand with Stratford-on-Avon Company. Played a lead in "A Midsummer Night's Dream" on Broadway in 1951 and made film debut in "Angels One Five" in 1952.

Drusus
The Ambitious, blind to all save his petty dreams of greed.

ADI BERBER, rotund Austrian cafe owner, who was born in Vienna and is known in his native city as the proprietor of the finest restaurants on the Danube. A powerfully built giant of a man, made acting debut as circus performer in "Carnival," an American film produced in Europe. This led Sam Zimbalist and William Wyler to select him for BEN-HUR; but after film was completed, he returned to Vienna and his first love—operating a cafe.

Malluch
The Mighty, not even Roman
rture could destroy his strength.

LAURENCE PAYNE, who was born in London. Studied at Old Vic Dramatic School before making debut with Old Vic Theatre. Remained with this famous repertory group five years. Has had wide experience in Shakespearean drama and performed with great success at Stratford-on-Avon. Made film debut in "Train of Events" in 1946, and has played leading roles in many films and plays, and with the BBC repertory group.

Joseph
The Carpenter, who, with his wife Mary, came to Bethlehem.

Art Director Edward Carfagno (kneeling), Set Decorator Hugh Hunt (right), check over set sketches with Wyler

MANY women in Italy gave their hair for *Ben-Hur*. More than four hundred pounds were assembled at Cinecittà Studios to be made into wigs and beards required by the thousands of people taking part in the production.

Most of the hair came from the peasant women of Upper Piedmont. Natives of this mountainous district, long famous for their fine hair, for centuries have been selling their locks to wig-makers of the world.

It was necessary to train a blacksmith for the seventy-eight horses used in the film. It seems that the old-fashioned "village smithy" is fast becoming extinct. The company found an eighteen-year-old boy who had spent much of his life around horses. He was taught the blacksmith trade and added to the permanent staff.

The research staff on "Ben-Hur" included a leading Protestant, a Catholic and a Jewish religious authority.

When Director Wyler needed a parchment with Hebrew words for a scene, he consulted a professor at the University of Jerusalem. The latter copied a section of the Dead Sea Scrolls onto the parchment, since the period of the film coincides with the time the Scrolls are believed to have been written. The professor is one of the experts who, for the past several years, has been helping to decipher the Scrolls.

Two doctors and two nurses were on duty throughout the filming of the race sequence, maintaining a twenty-bed infirmary at the edge of the arena. While none of the drivers sustained serious injury, the staff was kept busy treating heat prostrations and minor illnesses among the fifteen thousand extras who jammed the stands.

During production, *Ben-Hur* played host to more than a score of famous show-business personalities. Among those who visited the set in Rome were Kirk Douglas, Susan Hayward, Jack Palance, Harry Belafonte, Perry Como, Mel Ferrer, Bette Davis, Audrey Hepburn, Alec Guinness, Ed Sullivan, Agnes Moorehead, Van Heflin, Richard Basehart, Valentina Cortese, Susan Kohner, Ava Gardner, Anna Magnani and Geoffrey Horne.

The entire mountain village of Arcinazzo, all three hundred inhabitants, turned to acting during the week the company filmed in the mountains nearby. The village, located one hundred miles from Rome, became the town of Nazareth, and all residents were drafted for roles.

A notice in Rome newspapers calling for men with beards to present themselves at the studio resulted in a near riot. In anticipation of such a call, Romans had started growing beards months before. More than five thousand showed up the day after the newspaper announcement appeared. Beards ranged from a mere stubble to one luxurious facial muff almost three feet in length.

Cinecittà Studios and the sets for Ben-Hur *became a regular daily tour for the sightseeing buses of Rome. They arrived on hourly schedules and were allowed to tour the lot. More than 25,500 tourists from all over the world viewed the production.*

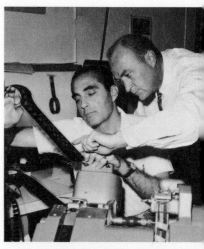

Film editors Ralph Winters (left) and Jack Dunning look over some of the 1,125,000 feet of exposed film.

Karl Tunberg at work on the script.

Shields in the wardrobe departme

In the seventh year of the reign of Augustus Caesar

. . . the people of Judea were ordered to return to the places of their birth to be counted and taxed. Among them were Joseph of Nazareth and his wife, Mary.

Arriving late, they found shelter in the stables of an inn. There, in a manger, a Child was born to Mary . . .

From Rome comes the young Tribune, Messala, to take command of the military garrison in Jerusalem.

Ben-Hur, with his mother and sister, entertains his boyhood friend, Messala, whom he has not seen in many years.

Even as Ben-Hur and Messala drink to their friendship, they begin to realize that in the future they will be enemies.

The slave, Esther, receives her freedom as a wedding gift from her master, Ben-Hur.

An anguished Ben-Hur pleads with Messala to release his family from imprisonment.

For one brief moment Ben-Hur holds the life of Messala in his hands, then relents, and is taken prisoner.

The thirst-crazed Ben-Hur is given water by a young carpenter's apprentice.

For three years Ben-Hur toils in the war galleys of Rome. Only his hate keeps him alive.

Churning oars drive the galleys to ramming speed as the Romans attack the Macedonian fleet.

Quintus Arrius, the Roman Commander, is knocked overboard at the climax of the great sea battle.

Ben-Hur and Arrius, whom he has saved from drowning, await rescue.

In Rome, Ben-Hur meets the beautiful Flavia and Pontius Pilate, the newly appointed Governor of Judea.

Sheik Ilderim reveals his plan [to] race his chariot against the Roma[ns] at the games held in Jerusale[m.]

Ben-Hur returns to his home and, from Esther and Simonides, tries to learn the fate of his mother and sister.

The trumpets sound. The chariots begin a parade to the starting line.

Past screaming thousands, around the turn of the Spina

The duel begins, as Messala lashes Ben-Hur across the face with his whip.

e nine chariots charge as the race gets under way.

In a desperate maneuver, Ben-Hur drives over the wreckage of two chariots.

Pilate awards the victor's crown of laurel.

Dying, Messala whispers the last of his hate.

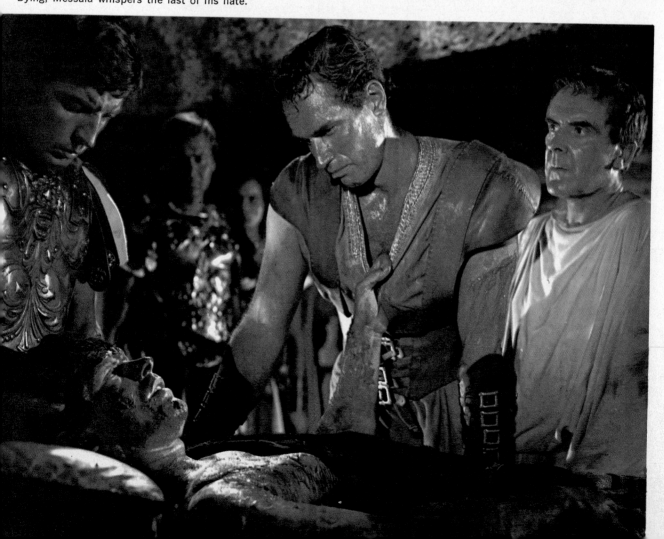

Sermon on
Mount.

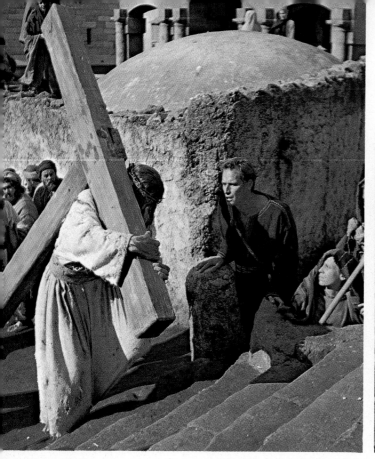

A tragic march.

On the hill at Calvary, Christ is crucified between two thiev

For Ben-Hur and Esther, a new day begins—for the world, a new era.

THE July day was hot. The Italian sun beat down on the two men with the intensity of a blast from a flaming furnace. Standing in the courtyard of a lavish Roman villa, they spoke to each other, at first softly, then in voices rising to a shrill crescendo.

When they had finished, a short, stocky man who had been listening with fierce concentration spoke:

"Let's do it once more, please."

Charlton Heston and Stephen Boyd, the two men, forgot the heat and discomfort of the heavy costumes they were wearing. For the twentieth time they proceeded to speak their lines for Scene 65-A in *Ben-Hur*.

It never occurred to them to complain. William Wyler, the director, had asked for "one more."

As anyone who has ever worked on one of his films knows, what William Wyler demands any actor is ready and willing to give—with no questions asked. It was enough for Heston and Boyd to know Wyler felt the scene could be improved. From experience they knew he would settle for nothing less than perfection.

Known as one of the most painstaking and meticulous directors in the business, William Wyler literally has actors fighting to work for him. Charlton Heston, like many others, says he'll gladly appear in any Wyler film without seeing the script.

William Wyler uses finder to line up scene with cameraman Robert Surtees.

Probably no other director has ever been so honored, nor so roundly praised by critics and public alike. A two-time winner of the coveted Academy Award for best screen direction of the year, he has been nominated for the award thirteen times—ten times as a director and three times as a producer.

Mrs. Miniver and *The Best Years of Our Lives* were the two films which won him Oscars. Others for which he received nomination for best direction were: *Dodsworth* (1936), *Wuthering Heights* (1939), *The Letter* (1940), *The Little Foxes* (1941), *The Heiress* (1949), *Detective Story* (1951), *Roman Holiday* (1952), and *Friendly Persuasion* (1956). Of the six pictures which he produced as well as directed, three were nominated for the "Best Picture of the Year" award.

Among the players who have received Oscars for performances under Wyler's direction are Audrey Hepburn, Bette Davis, Greer Garson, Olivia de Havilland, Fredric March, Teresa Wright, Walter Brennan and Harold Russell. Twenty-one others have received nominations.

The current *Ben-Hur* is not Wyler's first association with General Wallace's story. When Metro-Goldwyn-Mayer produced a silent version of the novel he was one of the more than thirty assistant directors assembled from all over Hollywood to guide the extras into the arena during the filming of the famous chariot race.

He had come to California in 1922 to work as a prop boy and a script clerk at the Universal Studios, then presided over by Carl Laemmle. Wyler, born in Mulhouse in Alsace, France (his father was Swiss, his mother German), had met Laemmle on one of the latter's frequent trips to Europe. The older man, impressed by the youth's energy and his intelligence, gave him a job in Universal's New York office.

He left this post to try his luck in Hollywood. In 1928, he began directing Western films, turning them out at a rate of one a week on a budget of $2,000 each (about the cost of an hour's work on one of the big scenes in *Ben-Hur*).

William Wyler, who has created a number of the most outstanding motion pictures ever produced, reaches the pinnacle of his genius with *Ben-Hur*.

Driving his Italian Vespa, William Wyler arrives on Ben-Hur set in Rome ready for another day's work on the picture.

CASTING

Thousands of extras who appear in the film file into Cinecittà Studios at 6 A.M. They were divided into groups, each with special number and letters. On several occasions more than twice as many extras turned up as could be used and police had to be called to prevent riot

METRO-GOLDWYN-MAYER opened a casting office in Rome in mid-1957 to select the more than fifty thousand persons who would appear in *Ben-Hur*.

Literally from the far corners of the world came the men, women, boys and girls who appeared in front of the six cameras used to film the spectacular story.

Of the many thousands finally selected, a total of three hundred and sixty-five had to speak lines. Forty-five were considered sufficiently important to be listed as principals.

The names of those in top roles read like a United Nations roll call.

Only four of the stars (Heston, Miss Scott, Miss O'Donnell and Jaffe) were born in the United States or had worked in Hollywood. The others came from such widely separated places as Israel, North Wales, Australia, Ireland, England, Austria and Italy.

Among those with small but important roles are such varied personalities as Claude Heater, a Californian who has gained fame singing with leading opera companies in Europe; Count Mario Rivoltella, whose great-great grandfather invented the revolver; Tom O'Leary, a Punxsutawney, Pennsylvania, youth, who has been studying opera in Italy; Tiberio Mitri, one-time heavyweight boxing champion of Europe; Tutti Lemkow, famous Norwegian ballet dancer; Guiseppe Tosi, once bodyguard to Italy's King Victor Emmanuel, and six prominent cowboy actors from Hollywood who traveled more than six thousand miles to drive in the chariot race.

Members of Rome's aristocracy lined up for work, with every day bringing at least a Count or a Baroness to the casting-office door. They were ready and waiting when Director Wyler decided he wanted genuine patricians to portray guests at an elaborate party. Among those who answered the seven A.M. call for this sequence were Prince Emanuele Ruspoli, of Italy, and his brother Prince Raimondo; Count Santiago Oneto, of Spain; Prince and Princess Hohenlohe, of Austria; Princess Irina Wassilchikoff, of Russia; Count Marigliano del Monte, of Italy; Baroness Lillian de Balzo of Hungary; and Duchess Nona Medici of Italy.

No Clash of Accents

Wyler's determination not to have a clash of accents resulted in his decision to use only Britishers to portray ancient Romans, with Americans for the most part taking the roles of the Hebrews.

Days before each big scene was scheduled to go before the cameras, the casting department began notifying extras, all of whom had been catalogued previously. The problems become obvious when it is considered that more than eighty-five percent of those who applied had no telephone by which they could be contacted and many had no address, but had merely indicated that they could be reached through such and such a friend.

As the mob extras were engaged, they were placed in the charge of a more experienced extra who, thereafter, would be responsible for getting those in his group to work on time. It was also his duty to see that his unit, usually thirty in number, moved in and out of make-up promptly. Some thirty water boys, in costume, circulated among the extras to ladle out water in plastic cups with which each extra was supplied.

In order to handle the large mobs of people without confusion (more than fifteen thousand alone for the chariot race), it was necessary for the first unit to move into wardrobe not later than five in the morning and often the last group would not be cleared until ten at night.

For the comfort and convenience of these extras and bit players, the studio built and maintained a "high speed" restaurant which, at its peak, fed five thousand extras in twenty minutes!

IT was decided by Metro-Goldwyn-Mayer more than five years ago to produce *Ben-Hur* on a scale that could not have been dreamed about prior to the new and highly advanced techniques of film-making which have been developed during the past decade.

This would be *Ben-Hur* at its ultimate, an entertainment achievement that might truly have caused General Wallace to exclaim: "Did I set all this in motion?"

Sam Zimbalist, whose productions of *King Solomon's Mines, Mogambo,* and *Quo Vadis* had helped make screen history, was selected to produce. By any standards—experience, temperament or talent—he was considered one of Hollywood's foremost movie-makers. Known for the courage and vision with which he attempted new fields of entertainment, he was responsible for several dozen memorable motion pictures. His untimely death occurred in Rome during the last stages of the production to which he had devoted so many years.

After the selection of Zimbalist as producer, a survey was made to determine the best locales for filming. Because of other productions at work at the Metro-Goldwyn-Mayer Studios in California, it was necessary to make the film abroad.

After investigating facilities in France, Spain, Italy, Mexico and England, it was decided to lease the vast Cinecittà Studios, eight miles from downtown Rome.

Its one hundred and forty-eight acres and nine large sound stages— the largest motion picture plant in Europe—have been equipped by the Italian government with the most modern technical apparatus.

The wheels at Metro-Goldwyn-Mayer, half a globe away, were already turning.

For the more than three hundred

Sol C. Siegel, Metro-Goldwyn-Mayer production chief, and leading lady, Haya Harareet.

sets to be built, a torrent of fifteen thousand sketches began pouring from the Studio's art department. Photostatic copies of these were catalogued for others engaged in preliminary production preparations.

A full two years before a camera was to turn, a skeleton staff of technicians arrived in Rome to begin supervision on construction of sets and the many additional buildings that would be needed. They were under the supervision of Henry Henigson, veteran Hollywood production genius.

It was during this period, too, that several hundred tons of equipment, including six of the newly developed Camera 65 units, each valued at $100,000, were loaded aboard two ships in California. This vast arsenal of technical material arrived in Italy well in advance of the official starting

Producer Sam Zimbalist on the Ben-Hur set in Italy.

Charlton Heston and his leading lady, Haya Harareet, stroll between scenes on the set in Rome.

date, which had now been established by Joseph R. Vogel, president of Loew's, Incorporated, for May, 1958.

Dominating the studio back lot was the arena for the chariot race sequence. Covering more than eighteen acres, with fifteen-hundred-foot straightaways alongside a Spina in the center, this was the largest single motion picture set ever built. Four statues atop the Spina stood thirty feet high. Into the arena went close to a million feet of lumber, more than a million pounds of plaster and two hundred and fifty miles of metal tubing. Sturdy enough to hold thousands of persons, the stands reached five stories high, every

inch covered with special fire-proofing material.

No one sequence of the film required more planning than the race. A full six months before an actor arrived in Rome, seventy-eight horses from Yugoslavia and Sicily had been assembled and were being trained by Glenn Randall, famed Hollywood animal expert. A veterinarian, a blacksmith, a harness-maker and twenty stable boys were engaged. Other experienced horsemen were brought from the United States to assist. The horses, a number of them Lippizaners, were conditioned and trained as if they were being prepared to run the Kentucky Derby, the Preakness and the Grand National—all in one day.

A training area of the same dimensions as the arena was built near the stables, and it was here the horses were put through their paces by Andrew Marton and Yakima Canutt, who had been selected to be the sec-

ond unit directors.

Three months went into the actual filming of the race, one of the most thrilling sequences ever recorded.

Other large sets were built at the studio and a man-made lake was dug and two full-sized galleys placed upon it for close shots of the sea battle sequence. More than two score ships were built for the long shots of the battle.

Additional scenes were filmed in the mountains near Arcinazzo, on the sands near the sea at Anzio and at a number of other sites in Italy.

Thousands upon thousands of costumes (it was impossible to make an accurate count) were assembled from all over the world. Bolts of rare silk, for instance, were procured from Thailand.

More than a million props to decorate the sets were assembled by a staff that began work in Rome two

Christopher Fry, noted poet-playwright, who was on set throughout production, confers with Mr. Wyler on dialogue.

Charlton Heston works out with horses brought from Yugoslavia for chariot race sequence.

years before the picture started. Eighteen chariots, nine to be used in the film, the others for practice, were built by the ancient coach-making firm, the Danesi Brothers of Rome.

From the start, Zimbalist and Metro-Goldwyn-Mayer were determined to have William Wyler, universally recognized as one of the finest directors the screen has ever known, guide the huge project. Wyler saw in *Ben-Hur* the challenge of his career. It was the movingly dramatic story and its colorful characters, as well as its grandeur and spectacle, that excited him.

Wyler and Zimbalist actually went to the far corners of the world to gather the principal actors and actresses to head the cast of thousands appearing in front of the camera.

Charlton Heston, one of the foremost actors of screen, stage and television, was considered the perfect choice for the exacting title role. As Ben-Hur, he appears in all but a dozen scenes of the film. England's Jack Hawkins, Ireland's Stephen Boyd, Israel's Haya Harareet, Wales' Hugh Griffith; America's Martha Scott, Cathy O'Donnell, and Sam Jaffe; Australia's Frank Thring; England's Finlay Currie and the many others selected for leading roles were regarded as ideal for their parts.

The screen play of *Ben-Hur* becomes a lasting monument to the talents of Karl Tunberg, one of Hollywood's most experienced and successful writers. Other great creative writers worked on the film. Distinguished playwrights Maxwell Anderson, S. N. Behrman and Gore Vidal all made important contributions. To top this rare array of writing talent came Christopher Fry, recognized as one of the great poet-playwrights of contemporary literature. Mr. Fry was on the set at Director Wyler's side throughout the production in Rome. It is the first time he has worked on a motion picture.

Sol C. Siegel, whose name has become synonymous with fine motion pictures, as production head of Metro-Goldwyn-Mayer Studios, acted as overseer of the entire project, giving it the stamp of his fine creative taste.

Producer Sam Zimbalist (right) and Director Wyler in front of a camera during the filming of an important scene.

THE SETS

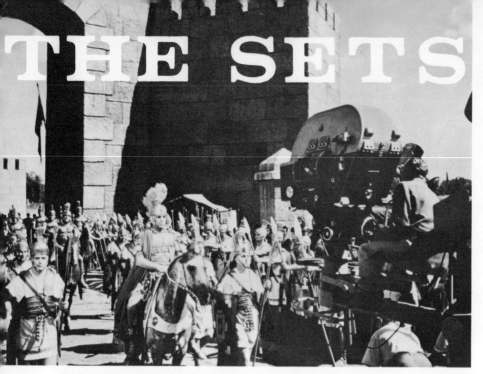

Camera 65 photographs Messala leading the Roman troops into Jerusalem.

IF you had been in Rome in 1958 or 1959 you would, like all good tourists, have visited St. Peter's, the Colosseum, and the other historic landmarks with which the Eternal City abounds. But your sightseeing would not have ended there.

Typical of the thousands of tourists in Rome during this period, you would have boarded a blue-and-white trolley, hopped on a bus or scrambled into a taxi and headed for the plains at the foot of the Alban Hills on the outskirts of the city.

The magnet? . . . Cinecittà Studios where *Ben-Hur* was being filmed.

Cinecittà, with one hundred and forty-eight acres and nine large sound stages, was built in 1936. It has been used as a factory for Italian war materiel during World War II, a barracks for German soldiers, and later as a sanctuary for thirty thousands of displaced persons from all over Europe.

Months before the cameras turned on *Ben-Hur* the studio was undergoing transformations tailored to suit the filming of this story. Plans for the production's three hundred sets, interiors and exteriors, were mapped on drawing boards. One of the largest sound stages was converted into a warehouse for the storage of costumes; another was divided into a dry-cleaning plant, a laundry, a shoe repair shop, and a gallery where sculptors created the two hundred

pieces of statuary needed for the sets in the film.

On this acreage some of the largest sets in the history of film-making were constructed. Dominating these was the arena, scene of the famous chariot race. Modeled after the ancient circus in Jerusalem, its construction kept more than one thousand workmen occupied for a year carving its graceful oval from a rock quarry which covered eighteen acres at the far end of the studio property.

As a tourist you would have been both impressed and interested in such arena statistics as:

> Close to 1,000,000 feet of lumber,
> 1,000,000 pounds of plaster,
> 250 miles of metal tubing,
> 40,000 tons of white sand, imported from nearby Mediterranean beaches.

Next port of call was a dock where Roman galleys were moored. These galleys were modeled after actual plans unearthed in various Italian museums.

Next the tourist would have been dazzled by the sight of the elaborate Roman villa of Quintus Arrius. Forty-five fountains fed through 8.9 miles of special pipe provided the background for the colorful party hosted by Arrius.

Covering a twenty-block area, complete with homes and business districts, the set representing the streets of Jerusalem was large enough to accommodate thousands. A feature of this set was the huge Gate of Joppa, reaching seventy-five feet into the sky.

On one hundred and forty-eight acres, art directors William Horning and Edward Carfagno created the glory that was Rome, and the grandeur that was Jerusalem.

It took three hundred sets, five years of research, and fourteen months of labor to turn back the historical clock to the years 1 A.D. and 31 A.D. And while modern Romans went about their work outside the gates, the ghosts of their ancestors trod within, retracing the steps of one of the greatest stories ever told.

One of the big scenes, this one at the Joppa Gate, in the spectacular picture.

To gather the wardrobe for a motion picture of the size and scope of *Ben-Hur* involves the sort of logistics that would make an army quartermaster quail. A staff of more than one hundred in Rome began the task almost a year before the production was to start. And through it were affected the economies of many nations, among them Germany, England, Yugoslavia, Italy and far away Thailand.

Vast sums were spent in manufacturing costumes by the thousands, which would appear in the picture. And the job had to begin early in order to have everything ready when the starting date arrived.

That is why Thailand natives started spinning silks for the clothes to be worn by the principals, and English workers were embroidering woolens and tooling leathers. In Italy they were creating boots, thick of sole and reaching to the knee. In Germany they were manufacturing elegant armor.

From South America came more

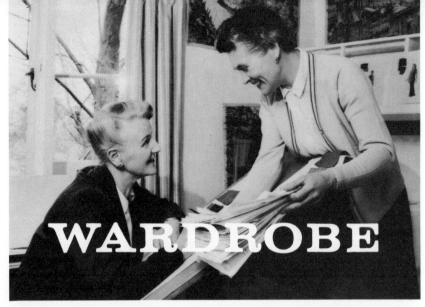

WARDROBE

Elizabeth Haffenden, Costume Designer, and Joan Bridge (right), Costume Color Consultant, check some of the thousands of wardrobe sketches made for the film.

woolens, from Switzerland, pieces of rare costume jewelry, from France, bolts of lace.

This huge inventory of clothes and accompanying accessories were assembled in three buildings at the Cinecittà Studios. Here seamstresses, leather workers, armorers, dry-cleaning experts worked many months to keep the vast wardrobe in good condition.

Elizabeth Haffenden, noted British designer, and her collaborator, Joan Bridge, color expert, created more than eight thousand separate sketches and drawings. The costumes that resulted not only are visually beautiful, but are considered by many to be the most authentic ever used in a picture.

More than two years of research preceded the writing of the music score for *Ben-Hur*—two years of delving through the musty files of the libraries of the world.

Written and conducted by the world famous Dr. Miklos Rozsa, the score adheres to the musical knowledge of Ben-Hur's day, in many cases using the homophonous chants of the early Greeks and Romans in which everything is played or sung in unison. One of the great problems was to make the music sound archaic without being grating to the ear.

It took seventy-two hours and twelve recording sessions to translate the score to the screen, and it emerges the longest ever composed for a motion picture. It was recorded in six channel stereophonic sound by the hundred-piece M-G-M Symphony Orchestra under the baton on Dr. Rozsa.

The score, which embraces a wide range of composition, is notable for many moods, especially the marches, three of which were composed for the production. One is played during the triumphal entry of the Roman legions into Jerusalem; one is background for the victory march of Quintus Arrius into Rome; the third is a prelude to the thrilling chariot race. Greek and Sicilian melodies form the basis for these compositions.

While Dr. Rozsa made no deliberate attempt to compose thematic phrases for the various characters in *Ben-Hur,* he did create a love theme for harp and flute, introduced at the first meeting of Ben-Hur and Esther.

Another highly effective use of instrumentation is the transition from full orchestra to organ during the sequences in which the Christ appears.

The rare and unusual score is being recorded in both stereo and monaural albums. Metro-Goldwyn-Mayer Records, alone, has issued three separate albums with Rozsa conducting.

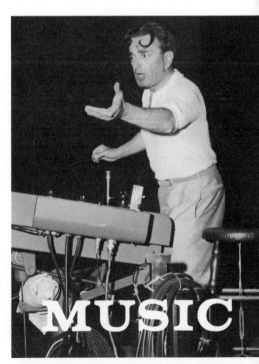

MUSIC

Miklos Rozsa conducts the Metro-Goldwyn-Mayer Symphony Orchestra in the score he has created for the film.

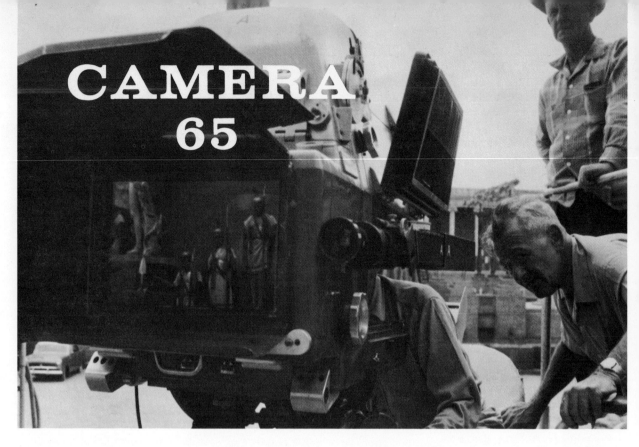

CAMERA 65

THE past few years have witnessed many notable advancements in wide-screen filming and projection techniques—all aimed at a greater sense of audience participation in action on the screen.

In filming *Ben-Hur*, Metro-Goldwyn-Mayer was determined to have the most exciting photography obtainable. Indeed, the wide sweep and grandeur of its spectacular scenes, as well as the importance of its more intimate sequences, made it mandatory that the most dramatic pictorial method be used.

That is why it was decided to use the recently developed Metro-Goldwyn-Mayer Camera 65, for a new and vastly improved motion picture image.

The process incorporates a number of new concepts for presentation of the sharpest, most brilliant image ever seen on the screen. As the name implies, Camera 65 uses film which is sixty-five millimeters wide (over two-and-a-half inches). It covers an area two hundred and seventy-five percent larger than conventional thirty-five millimeter film, and this is what helps produce the unusually clear, bright definitions and smooth, grainless texture of the images.

Six of these costly cameras (with their rare lenses, they are valued at more than $100,000 each) were shipped to Rome.

Development of the Camera 65 project was under the supervision of technical researchers at Metro-Goldwyn-Mayer. Optical equipment was produced, after intensive research, by Panavision, Inc., under the personal guidance of President Robert E. Gottschalk. The design, skill and manufacturing experience, which have made this California company the world's largest producer of specialized optical equipment for theatre use, contributed in large measure to the remarkable new lens systems.

In them, Panavision incorporated a spherical type "objective" lens manufactured from so-called "rare earth" glasses and an anamorphic element which imparts a slight horizontal squeeze to the images on the film. This squeeze is removed by the projection lens and the image appears distortion free and normal on the screen.

The overall depth and the high quality of picture produced by these unique lenses allows the audience to feel it is seeing the actual scene through an open window, rather than an image on a screen.

A unique feature of Camera 65 is the complete flexibility of the large negative which can be printed to any size exhibition film. It is adaptable to the projection methods and facilities of *all* other systems now in use. It is also adaptable to whatever further variations of screen size or aspect ratio may develop.

In Rome, Robert Surtees, long recognized as one of Hollywood's most skillful cinematographers, headed a large unit, composed of some of the finest cameramen from the United States, Italy and England. Operating under extremely difficult conditions, they sometimes used as many as five separate cameras at the same time. On the sands at Anzio and in the mountains of Northern Italy, they mounted a unit on the huge Chapman boom and moved into areas never explored by a camera.

Ben-Hur, all experts agree, is ideally suited for presentation in this exciting new Camera 65 process. Its scenes could not have reached full pictorial potential in any other medium.

THE CAST

JUDAH BEN-HUR	Charlton Heston	LEPER	Tutte Lemkow
QUINTUS ARRIUS	Jack Hawkins	HORTATOR	Howard Lang
MESSALA	Stephen Boyd	CAPTAIN, RESCUE SHIP	Ferdy Mayne
ESTHER	Haya Harareet	DOCTOR	John Le Mesurier
SHEIK ILDERIM	Hugh Griffith	BLIND MAN	Stevenson Lang
MIRIAM	Martha Scott	BARCA	Aldo Mozele
SIMONIDES	Sam Jaffe	STARTER AT RACE	Thomas O'Leary
TIRZAH	Cathy O'Donnell	CENTURION	Noel Sheldon
BALTHASAR	Finlay Currie	OFFICER	Hector Ross
PONTIUS PILATE	Frank Thring	SOLDIER	Bill Kuehl
DRUSUS	Terence Longden	MAN IN NAZARETH	Aldo Silvani
SEXTUS	André Morell	VILLAGER	Diego Pozzetto
FLAVIA	Marina Berti	MARCELLO	Dino Fazio
TIBERIUS	George Relph	RAIMONDO	Michael Cosmo
MALLUCH	Adi Berber	CAVALRY OFFICER	Aldo Pini
AMRAH	Stella Vitelleschi	DECURIAN	Remington Olmstead
MARY	Jose Greci	GALLEY OFFICER NO. 1	Victor De La Fosse
JOSEPH	Laurence Payne	GALLEY OFFICER NO. 2	Enzo Fiermonte
SPINTHO	John Horsley	MARIO	Hugh Billingsley
METELLUS	Richard Coleman	ROMAN AT BATH	Tiberio Mitri
MARIUS	Duncan Lamont	PILATE'S SERVANT	Pietro Tordi
AIDE TO TIBERIUS	Ralph Truman	THE CORINTHIAN	Jerry Brown
GASPAR	Richard Hale	THE BYZANTINE	Otello Capanna
MELCHIOR	Reginald Lal Singh	THE SYRIAN	Luigi Marra
QUAESTOR	David Davies	THE LUBIAN	Cliff Lyons
JAILER	Dervis Ward	THE ATHENIAN	Edward J. Auregui
THE CHRIST	Claude Heater	THE EGYPTIAN	Joe Yrigoyan
GRATUS	Mino Doro	THE ARMENIAN	Alfredo Danesi
CHIEF OF ROWERS	Robert Brown	OLD MAN	Raimondo Van Riel
ROWER NO. 42	John Glenn	SEAMAN	Mike Dugan
ROWER NO. 43	Maxwell Shaw	SPORTSMAN	Joe Canutt
ROWER NO. 28	Emile Carrer		

BEN-HUR

Produced by	Sam Zimbalist	Film Editors	Ralph E. Winters, A.C.E.
			John D. Dunning, A.C.E.
Directed by	William Wyler	2nd Unit Directors	Andrew Marton
Screen Play by	Karl Tunberg		Yakima Canutt
Music by	Miklos Rozsa		Mario Soldati
Director of Photography	Robert L. Surtees, A.S.C.	Assistant Directors	Gus Agosti
Additional Photography	Harold E. Wellman, A.S.C.		Alberto Cardone
	Pietro Portalupi	Make-up by	Charles Parker
Art Directors	William A. Horning	Unit Production Manager	Edward Woehler
	Edward Carfagno	Recording Supervisor	Franklin Milton
Set Decorations	Hugh Hunt	Sound Recordists	Sash Fisher, A.M.I.E.E.
Special Effects	A. Arnold Gillespie		William Steinkamp
	Lee LeBlanc	Costumes designed by	Elizabeth Haffenden
	Robert R. Hoag, A.S.C.	Color Consultant—Costumes	Joan Bridge
Color Consultant—Settings	Charles K. Hagedon	Hair Styles by	Gabriella Borzelli

BEN STAHL, the noted American artist, has created a series of extraordinary paintings depicting his conception of memorable moments in BEN-HUR. These reproductions are arranged so that they may be removed for framing. →

May be removed from the book by cutting carefully along the dotted line.

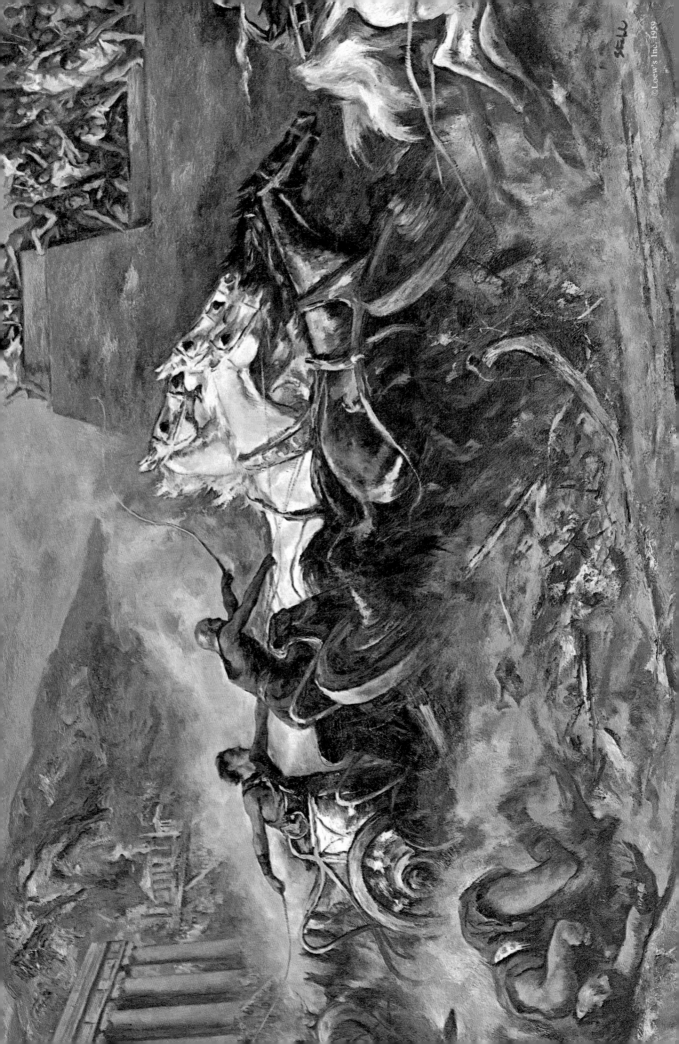